Idea to Print

The Step-By-Step Guide to Kick Writer's Block's Butt and Finally Finish and Publish Your Book

Katelyn Silva

Access the *Idea to Print* Bonus Package

As a huge thank you for checking out *Idea to Print*, I put together a special bonus package with free resources and training as you're going through the book. Make sure you get yours!

Go to:
wewritebooks.com/i2pbonus

Ready to Write & Publish *Your* Book?

Write. Publish. Inspire.

There is a ton of information in this book to give you what you need as you embark on the journey of becoming an author. Before you dive in, I'd like to preface by sharing that my hope is that you join my community further and engage in all there is to offer.

I want you to know that you're not in this alone.

In this book, I've held nothing back and you can definitely take it, implement, and finally reach your author goals. In fact, many before you have!

Many others have started to implement and realized they would love to have guidance and support through the journey. Some others have decided they just want it done for them.

Take just a moment, right now, close your eyes, and envision seeing your book, with your name, on your bookshelf.

Can you see it?

Now immerse yourself in all of the emotions that vision evokes.

I would love nothing more than to help you make that vision a concrete reality. I have various levels of support, depending on your needs as you dive into the journey.

Whatever that is for you, you're invited to a complimentary chat with me to dig into your vision, as well as where you've been struggling, to map out a clear plan forward to reach your goals, and ultimately determine your best next step in working with me.

Take advantage of this opportunity here:

wewritebooks.com/chat

Acknowledgements

This book has been a challenging one for me, despite my previous works. I struggled with some of the exact roots of writer's block I discussed within the book, such as self-doubt.

I kept asking myself, "Who am I to write this? Why is it better than any of the other countless books out there on writing and publishing? What do I *really* have to offer?"

Over the course of writing the book, I began to see that what makes this book special is that it offers things that I learned through my struggles and journey that are unique to me.

One of the big things I share with clients is that no one else in the world can share *your story, your way, with your experiences*. That is true for me and this book also.

It also illuminates how no writer is *alone*. There are some fantastic resources and books out there on writing and publishing, and I by no means claim that this book is exhaustive, but it does have what you need to realistically and practically finish and publish, if you do the work.

Having shared that, I'd like to take a moment and give a huge thank you and shout out to the people who rooted for me, encouraged me, and without whom I would've taken even longer to finish.

First and foremost is my friend Vinita Temmert, founder of *The MindShift Academy* and an amazing coach who truly helps people to make dramatic changes in their mind and life – and who lives this out every day by example. Vinita, you're amazing.

I'd also like to thank my editor Jake Waller for his patience with me taking my precious time finishing this; my two younger sisters Kirsten and Elsie, who constantly encourage my writing endeavors and ideas; and finally my amazing community of writers, for whom I specifically wrote this with the aim of providing something straight-forward and informative to help them accomplish their own writing and publishing goals.

Table of Contents

Introduction

Ever since I was a little girl... for as long as I can remember, I've loved writing.

It's what thrills me, what excites me, what settles me and relieves my stress. It's one of the things that drives me.

Even more than my own journey, I absolutely feel a fire when I see someone else's journey. When I see them light up about their own stories, ideas, and the books they want to create.

Most of all, I think that writing for me connects me to my mom. It's a piece of her that I will always carry with me no matter what. She was the one that gave me my love for writing. And it's a way that I can make her proud.

She began by teaching me to read *through* writing. I still remember writing letters to my dad while he was at work, and then having to wait for him to get home so he could read them back to me because I was still learning to read what I had written. Those are some of the happiest memories of my life.

She passed away when I was eight, and shortly after that, I became an avid reader. I buried myself in books, absolutely captivated by the stories within. Authors that truly impacted me include Tamora Pierce (at the top of the list), Walter Farley, J.R. Tolkien, C.S. Lewis, and Laura Ingles Wilder.

As I grew older, I got really involved in writing communities. The people I met during that time remain some of the most important friends to me. People that "get it". They understand the passionate love for writing, for creating.

During that time, I dabbled in writing my own books, but didn't ever see one to completion. At least not then.

At that time, it was just fun. It was coping with the realities of my life helping to raise three younger siblings, take care of the house, and stay on top of my own grades and extra-curricular activities.

It was also my escape from the never-ending chain of new girlfriends for my dad or new step-moms. I couldn't tell you the number of girlfriends, but I had three step-moms just during high school.

Regardless, writing was my constant. Imagination was my freedom.

I took a hiatus when I was eighteen. After making some bad decisions that ended in the darkest time of my life and becoming a single mom, I moved halfway across the country to do something different. To get on my feet, and do whatever it might take to give my son a good life. I worked hard, became a thriving restaurant manager, met my husband, got married, had another baby... by all accounts I was on the path to success.

But there was something missing.

The lack of writing was like a punch to the gut. I *needed* to write again. So I did. I finished my first book within six months, and within another year of grueling edits, it was published with a small publisher (when I still knew nothing of the publishing industry).

It was a total flop, but it was the beginning of my journey as an author.

Since then, I've gone on to write and publish three more novels and two short-stories, published in anthologies (all the fiction published under a pen name).

With each work, I grew. I learned something new, got a little bit better, and expanded my reach and my author platform.

This book is about how I did it. And how you can do it too.

If you have always felt like you had a story inside of you, a book you wanted to write, but you've never quite figured out where to start, or how to take that next step and publish, then this book is for you. I hope you find the information within to be helpful, insightful, and actionable.

I know that you can do this!

Over the course of the book, I'm going to take you from start to finish on how you can write your book and successfully become an author.

No matter if you're at the very beginning, or you're later on in your book, I promise that you will find useful tips and information!

If you'd like, you can skip to the point in the book where you feel you need to start (based on your writing journey), but if you read through the whole thing, follow my advice, and do the work, I guarantee you'll pick up some new ideas and walk away with a published book to be proud of.

As a quick disclaimer, this book is not exhaustive and does not go into detail on special techniques for specific genres. However, regardless of which genre you may be writing, the content within does provide practical, proven methods to accomplish writing and publishing your book.

Also, as we get to the publishing stage, much of the content is geared toward self-publishing, as after experiencing both, I've become an advocate for self, since I believe it provides far more flexibility and benefits for authors in today's industry.

However, even if your heart is set on following the traditional route, I encourage you to read through these sections, as you'll still gain insights for completing your book as well as food for thought as you set out on the publishing portion of your journey.

As you're reading the book, I encourage you to pause, take action, and then come back for each step of the process. I'm sharing the steps I use for each and every one of my books, but they'll only work for you if you put them into action.

In this way, not only will you have guidance during each part of the process, but you'll never be alone. So, let's get your book finished and published!

Part I

Turn Your Idea into a Completed Book

Chapter 1
The Five Root Causes of Writer's Block (and How to Weed Them Out)

Before we dive in to the actual writing, I want to get two major things out of the way. If you struggle with finding *time* to write, let alone writing itself, there will be some specific tips in this book ahead, but I also have a quick read and a guide that can help you find time for your writing in order to get it done. You can access both inside the special *Idea to Print* Bonus Package:

wewritebooks.com/i2pbonus

The second major thing is... I want to completely eliminate any writer's block you may be dealing with. (And how to deal with it if it tries to come back!)

Writer's block is like a weed sprouting up and trying to choke out the beautiful flower of your imagination and your great ideas. In order to truly eliminate the weed and allow your flower to flourish, you must first get to the roots and then remove all traces.

This chapter is all about the roots of writer's block. Once you identify what they are, you can eradicate them and if they try to come back, you'll overcome them with more ease each time.

I think every writer has faced or at least knows what writer's block is. At its simplest, it's dealing with 'blank-page syndrome'... staring at the blank page, cursor flashing and no words flowing!

But really, the block can come in many forms and stems from many places. We're going to dive into each one of them.

They include:

- Being outside of the creative flow zone (which results in trying to force the writing, losing motivation, or even avoiding the writing altogether)

- Lack of direction and idea hopping (also leads to losing motivation, or feeling unclear on where to start)
- Others saying you can't do it (which contributes to, and even causes, the next two root-causes)
- Self-doubt
- Fear of failure, rejection, or even success

The Creative Flow Zone

If nothing else, this one thing can be huge for tackling writer's block and summoning the muse at will. Mastering your creative flow zone is a must.

If you're wondering what the heck this is, basically, every person has a natural, internal time-frame when their creativity is at its peak. For you, it might be 5am to 8am, or maybe it's 2pm-6pm, or maybe it's 8pm to 1am. The important thing is that you know when it is for *you*.

You may already know what I'm talking about. Many writers don't know when this time is because it happens during a time when they can't typically tap into it (such as while they are working their regular job or taking care of dinner and the family), but I can give you a quick way to figure out your zone.

If you're wondering how you can figure out when this time is... close your eyes for just a minute. Think about a time in the past when you sat down to write and the words just flowed. It was like something magical happened and your momentum just took off.

If this has happened for you in the past, especially if it was more than once, you may notice a trend or pattern in the time of day.

It doesn't necessarily have to be a time when you were writing. It could also be a time when you're most productive, have the most ideas, or have a sudden burst of inspiration (while you were maybe in the middle of something and couldn't act on it).

Do you have it?

This is your creative zone. It's where your personal magic can happen as a writer.

I know what you're thinking. "But Katelyn, I can't write during that time." Or "But, what if it doesn't work?"

That's where the next piece comes into play.

In the same exercise, thinking about when your writing just flowed, consider more than just the time of day. Now consider the surrounding factors. What were you doing? What music were you listening to? Were you drinking coffee? Or maybe tea? Had you just finished a jog or a drive and as soon as you got home, you were able to sit down and write (instead of doing something else)? Was there a routine, or was it when you changed it up and got out of the house?

Grab a notepad or maybe your phone and write down your answers. Whatever they are for you, these are the things that help to stimulate your muse. These are the things that help to tell your brain, "Hey, it's time to write. Let's get going!"

Doing these things, especially right before or at the beginning of your creative zone will activate your flow and allow you to write prolifically.

Now that you know how to demand the muse's attention, there's still the question of time. Right? Maybe you're constantly being interrupted during this time. Or maybe you have to work.

Whatever the thing is that pulls you away, I want you to ask yourself something. How important is writing this book to you? Is it something you could put off or give up? Or is it something that if you don't get it out of you, you'll go nuts!

Just like the things that are necessary for survival – eating, sleeping, time with loved ones, etc. – we all make time for the things that we think are the most important.

Writing has to be the same for you. You have to *make* time. You have to make your creative zone sacred.

Read that one again.

It could mean letting your family know that this is your time so that you won't have interruptions.

Or, if you typically are at work during that time, realize that you don't work every single day. You may have to tap into your zone on your days off.

But guess what? Some of the most prolific writers don't necessarily write every single day. They write when they're in their zone. And because they're writing in their zone, they get twice as much accomplished during that time and make up for the time not writing.

For some writers, they write every day, but at times that means they're writing outside of their creative zone, and they don't get as much accomplished.

Of course, that's not to say you shouldn't write unless it's in your zone, as that's not always realistic, and we're going to cover how to tackle getting writing done in other ways. However, the point is that as much as you *can* write in your creative zone, do.

Ultimately, you have to find what works for you. But once you know what that is... *do it.*

For more details on how you can master your time to get more writing done, do grab those free resources I mentioned previously! They've helped every one of my clients to eliminate time as an issue.

wewritebooks.com/i2pbonus

Now, I said that would give you some major writer's block butt-kicking, but there are still more pieces to the puzzle, such as knowing your path.

Lack of Direction and Idea Hopping

The first thing to really consider before your book begins is where your book is going. Even if you're a 'pantser' – someone who 'flies by the seat of their pants', or in other words, someone that doesn't plan at all –

even a little bit of foundation and direction can be monumentally helpful!

I've written works with minimal detail in planning, I've written works that have been somewhat planned, and I've heavily planned for others.

My best work was by far the work where I had at least a direction and an idea of the major points and end goal.

So, before you even start writing, it's good to do what I call 'idea development' or 'book development' and lay a strong foundation.

If you've heard the parable of the men that built their houses on sand and on rock... well, you get what I mean. You want a book that is solid. Not one where you get to the end only to discover it's full of plot holes and is falling apart.

We'll dive into far more detail on direction in the next chapter, but I did want to briefly discuss how this can contribute to writer's block.

The biggest problem that I've seen is when a writer does one (or both) of two things. One is when the writer gets lost at some point in the story and no longer can see where the story is going.

The other is when the writer constantly gets new ideas in the middle of a story and then has multiple unfinished stories and can't seem to get one completed. I call this 'idea-hopping'.

I want you to think of your book like a forest or maze you've never been through before. Without a map, you're going to get terribly lost, right?

Whether fiction or non-fiction, your book is the same. You need a guideline to be able to get all the way through it without steering off course and looking back wondering how you got to where you are and how to get back on track to finish it.

Then, once you have that guideline, it's important to use it and stick with it.

Of course, when writing a book, there's room for deviation. Sometimes, that just happens. The important thing is to stay on track with the overarching points of the book that take you from beginning, through the middle, and to the end.

The next thing to tackle is how to deal with new ideas (and inspiration for those ideas) that come up while you're in the midst of writing your book.

If you've ever been in the middle of writing something when all of a sudden, a new idea hits, complete with a wave of excitement and inspiration for it, you may currently have several unfinished works because you've been unable to actually complete one of them without getting distracted and consumed by these new ideas.

Perhaps when these new ideas hit, you often find it difficult to continue the book you were already working on. You find yourself stuck or your motivation for it has gone.

So how can you effectively save your new ideas *and* stick with your current work?

The best way I've found is to keep a dedicated notebook or a folder on your computer specifically for ideas you'd like to turn into books at some point during your writing career.

Each time a new idea comes up, especially in the moment when you have the most clarity and inspiration for that idea, go ahead and take that pause on your current work and write down or type out your new idea.

However, don't let yourself get carried away trying to write that book right now.

Instead, write down a summary of what you're thinking as well as any major points you already know you can use. In fact, you could even go ahead and make an outline if your idea is clear so you can come back to it later.

Write down any points in such a way that you're not writing the actual content yet, but you're giving yourself a detailed enough summary that you can confidently come back and remember where you were going with the point and dive right back into the content.

Finally, once you feel like you've adequately written down your idea in a way that you can return to later, put it aside in that special notebook or folder and refocus on your current work. After all, the only way to finish your book is to write it through to the end!

We'll discuss how to rejuvenate your inspiration for your current work if you're struggling to stick with it, but for now, let's dive into the next cause of writer's block: being told you can't do it, and how that leads to more root causes such as fear of failure and self-doubt.

The Nay-Sayers and How They Cause Fear and Self-Doubt

We've probably all had that moment when we're excitedly sharing our idea or our book and the person listening gets a glazed look in their eyes. They probably are trying to be polite and disguise their lack of interest, but we can sense it.

So we try to quickly finish up whatever we were saying and move on to other conversation with a little bit of a sting in our heart.

Maybe you've had nothing but supportive people and if so, fantastic! But if not, if you've ever had someone in your life who doesn't believe in you or maybe even tries to deter you from pursuing your writing dreams, this can plant seeds of serious doubt and instill a fear of failure which can create all kinds of blocks when you're trying to actually write your book.

Many times, these people are individuals who are close friends or family and they have good intentions – maybe trying to protect us from disappointment – but they don't realize how much their disbelief hurts, or that just a little bit of encouragement and belief *in* us might actually be the thing that helps us create huge success.

When you're sitting down to write, if you find that little voice whispering in your mind that what you're writing isn't good, that it'll never do well, or that readers won't enjoy it, it can literally prevent you from pushing forward with your book and making the progress you actually want to make.

Maybe you find yourself deleting everything you just wrote, believing it's crap, or completely scrapping that idea and trying to move on to another one you're excited about.

You need to know that all of those negative thoughts about your book are nothing more than untruths. Yes, they may become reality. But the thing is, you're sabotaging yourself by giving in to those worries and fears.

Whether that means you never actually give your book a chance or that, if you do publish, you never really do anything to get it out there... you're the one turning those fears into reality.

Instead of focusing on the possibility of failure, know that there's an equal, if not greater, possibility of success!

Yes, this particular book may not do well. But maybe it will! Approach it with a sense of adventure and discovery. And even if it doesn't do well, that's okay. You'll learn from it and your next book will do better!

The truth is that very few authors are immediately hugely successful after their first or even second work. And further, most big authors don't have huge success on every single one of their works either.

The beauty of writing is that it doesn't stop with just one – unless you want it to. It's something beautiful and continuous and you improve the longer you write.

My first book was a complete and total flop. It was embarrassing! Yet I knew that I couldn't ever give up writing, so I took with me everything I learned from that experience and did better with the next one and the next one until I finally reached the success I not only desired, but knew was possible.

As you're approaching writing your book, take a moment and think of the authors and books you've read that have meant something to you. Think of the ones that impacted you and inspired you to pursue writing in the first place.

At least one, if not all, of those authors most certainly faced challenges, writer's block, fears, struggles, and their own journey through failures before they at last reached the level of success they wanted.

But they didn't give up. They pushed through so that their work might reach their intended readers – including you!

Now think about who your intended readers are and what you want them to get out of your book. Do you want to teach them, inspire them, entertain them, or share something special with them?

If you don't take the chance to put yourself out there, your book won't be able to do any of those things.

I believe that your book deserves to be written, that you deserve to finish it, and that your potential readers deserve to read it.

For anyone in your life that's tried to put you down or made you doubt whether you could truly be a writer, you're not writing for them anyway, right? You're writing because you have a purpose, a goal, with your book. You're writing it for yourself and for your readers. So focus on that every time you sit down to write.

I mentioned that nay-sayers cause and contribute to both fear of failure or rejection and self-doubt, but self-doubt can come from so many different things in our lives.

Nay-saying people definitely contribute to self-doubt. Self-doubt also comes from areas in life that you may think have nothing to do with writing. Maybe in the past, you've struggled to accomplish things you set out to do, or you've had previous failures in other endeavors. Maybe you've struggled with some health issues that have prevented you from doing things you really wanted to or have had a lack of genuine support for your goals and dreams.

The thing here is that while we can't always completely cut these nay-saying people out of our lives, we can set boundaries that limit what we allow them to influence.

Equally, it is important to seek out the support that you need. It can be challenging to truly put aside your doubts and fears. They have a tendency of resurfacing in the challenging moments of pushing through and accomplishing goals, in this case your book.

So instead of trying to go it alone, the best way to tackle these fears is through a support system.

Writing a book shouldn't be a solo project. Ever notice that at the beginning of most books is an acknowledgements page? When you truly have encouragement and support for your book and your writing, it eradicates the fear of failure and rejection because the opposite is literally right beside you.

Maybe you're wondering where to go or how to get this support – maybe you don't have anyone in your life you can immediately think of that can provide this for you.

If so, it's a great idea to look into online communities or local groups you might be able to become involved in. Even having just one person – a friend, a mentor, a fellow writer – can make a huge difference. That person can offer encouragement, a kick in the butt when you need it, someone to bounce ideas off, and accountability to keep you on track.

There are tons of writers' Facebook groups, LinkedIn groups, and more. Make it a point to engage, share what you're working on or struggling with, get feedback, and don't forget to also give to others in the group as well!

It doesn't have to be all the time. It can be once a week if that works best for you, so that it's not overwhelming, but still supportive. Plus, this prevents you from getting distracted by social media.

I'd like to invite you, especially if you don't already have a community, to join The Writer's Club on Facebook, which is specifically focused on providing just the environment I mentioned. In it, I also share regular content to help you finish and publish your book. You can join in here:

www.facebook.com/groups/writersclubmembership

If you don't feel great about participating in a community and feel you'd benefit from a more one-on-one type relationship, consider looking for a writing buddy or mentor.

I can't express enough how huge this has been for me in my own journey. Having both a writing buddy and a mentor literally made the difference, for me, between having an unfinished manuscript collecting dust and a published book I was proud to have sitting on my shelf.

If you want to learn more about how I can support you as a mentor including weekly check-ins and step-by-step guidance so you can avoid common pitfalls and instead see your printed book on your shelf, visit:

wewritebooks.com/chat

Get the support you need, limit the nay-sayers, and choose to focus on the possibilities your book has instead of whether or not it will flop.

Now that we've tackled how to deal with writer's block and where it comes from, let's get to why we're here: writing and publishing your book!

Key Points from the Chapter:

- The five root causes of writer's block are:
    - Lack of creative flow zone
    - Lack of direction
    - Naysayers
    - Self-doubt
    - Fear

- Overcome them through intentional, undistracted time set aside for your writing, doing the pre-work to get clarity on your content, and surrounding yourself with the appropriate support for success

Chapter 2
Your Four Foundational Pillars for Success

The next step you must take before diving into the writing process is to lay an adequate foundation to set yourself up for success.

The truth is that, even though we've identified the causes of writer's block, how they hold you back, and how to overcome them, they will still try to come up throughout your writing process.

So it's important to also acquire the tools you'll need to give you clear direction as you're writing so that no matter what, you can keep going until your book hits the finish line.

There are four major pillars to this strong foundation and setting yourself up for success.

They are:

- Your roadmap
- Your setting
- Knowing your characters or audience
- Research

Your Roadmap

In high school, our teachers called this an outline, and while I've come to a place of understanding why an outline is important, it's so much more fun to call it a map!

I mentioned earlier that the best way to understand why this is important to your book is to imagine your book and the writing of it as a huge forest you've never been through before. Maybe you've explored parts of it, but you've never ventured through to the end and, without a roadmap, you'll stumble from the path and get lost.

You know what this feels like if you've ever started writing, and then found yourself somewhere in your book without clear direction of where to go next, let alone how to get to the end.

Whether your book is fiction or non-fiction, a roadmap will not only give you that clear direction, but it will allow you to dive right back into your book even if you take a break from it or are in and out of your zone when you're writing.

You'll be able to look at your map and say, "Yes, this is where I'm going next!" and then make it happen.

To create this roadmap for yourself, you likely already have some idea of its basic structure, but there are probably a few areas that are kind of blurry for you. So, just like you can get stuck if you just dive right into the writing, you can also get stuck in your outline.

The first step is therefore to get everything in your mind onto paper. This accomplishes two things.

One, instead of all your book content being a giant jumble in your mind, you can now clearly organize it and move things around so that it makes sense and has a flow.

Even if you have a sense of direction within your mind, there are aspects of your book that aren't clear, and getting everything onto paper will allow you to look at it in a new way.

Secondly, by writing everything down, you open up your mind to process and create new ideas so that any areas that aren't clear can have a chance to become clear.

Think of it like driving on a long stretch of road. As you move further along, things in the distance that you could kind of make out become clearer and things you hadn't even seen before come into view.

So, grab a notebook, some plain paper, or maybe even a giant poster board, and give yourself at least fifteen minutes of undistracted time. Write down the overall topic of your book in the middle and then start writing literally anything and everything related that pops into your mind.

It doesn't matter how silly, small, or insignificant an idea seems. Write it down. Keep going until you have absolutely nothing left coming to you about this particular book idea.

Often, you'll find that as you're writing down what you already have, seeing it on the paper will start to spark new ideas and connect things together.

Once you have everything written down, you can step away to let everything settle and your mind process both the release of ideas and any new ideas that are forming. Or, if you want to, you can go ahead and continue to the next step.

Go back through everything you wrote down and start organizing the content. There are several ways to organize it, so choose what makes sense for you.

Maybe that means color-coding content that will be in the same chapter or area of the book, maybe numbering each piece of content, or maybe even just re-writing what you wrote in order of how you would like it to be in your book.

As you do this, if any new ideas pop up, perhaps how you'd like to explain an idea for non-fiction or craft a scene for fiction, go ahead and jot down those notes to the side as well.

Once you've organized your content, your roadmap is complete. You can take it a step further and write it out in actual outline format, or maybe you draw it out like a real map, but either way, you now have a clear path through your book.

Your Setting

This pillar in particular is specific to fiction, though it can apply to some areas of non-fiction, such as a memoir – recounting memories and needing to recreate those stories clearly for your reader. Even with non-fiction, there is always a level of creativity and story-telling involved!

Your setting should always be more detailed than what actually goes in your book. The more in-depth you go, the more you can create an experience for your readers where they feel completely drawn in.

It should include era or time in history, the universe it's set in (ours with our laws or a fictional one where things work differently), physical aspects such as whether it's set in a city or a more rural location, the social status of the characters and how that impacts their speech, lifestyles, clothing, etc.

Take time to really map out the details so that as you move through the book, if you're not quite sure if something is appropriate to the setting, you have a reference to keep your content consistent throughout.

Knowing Your Characters or Audience

I'm going to separate these aspects, but the process is similar. Knowing these will drive the direction and voice or tone of your book.

If you're writing fiction, then knowing your characters inside and out is important because as your story develops, elements like how scenes connect together and especially the dialogue are driven by character personalities and the way they would naturally respond or react to something.

If you're writing non-fiction, knowing exactly who you are speaking to and what you want them to get out of your book impacts the way you approach your writing and what you share.

Fiction: Know Your Character

Have you ever been working on a story when, all of a sudden, it felt like it was writing itself or that your characters took over and wrote it for you?

Well, this is how easy writing your story can be when you know your characters inside and out.

That's not to say hiccups won't happen, or that you won't have to take over and steer their direction, but it will help you avoid plot mishaps from a character behaving how they shouldn't. Also, it can help with filling in small details of the story as you'll know just how your characters would naturally react or behave in different situations.

The best way to get to know your character is to find a way to make doing so fun. You could do a character interview, just for yourself, where you are as silly or serious with it as you want to be. You could create a full character profile, or even come up with a short back-story to really explore that character's development prior to the main events of your book.

Consider the basic things such as name and appearance, but also explore questions such as personality and where the character came from.

What's their history? What are the reasons for their thought-processes or behaviors? What has caused change in the character before or inspired them to take action? What are their goals and aspirations?

Go as deep as you can, but also remember not to make this an extra chore for yourself. It's massively beneficial to know your characters really well, but if you're struggling with figuring out certain aspects of the character, move on.

Again, this should be a fun activity that helps make writing your book easier!

Non-Fiction: Know Your Reader

Similar to knowing your character, knowing your audience is something that will affect your writing process for your book.

Knowing your reader is beneficial for both fiction and non-fiction, but definitely in non-fiction, it's important to have a clear idea of who will be reading your book. The reason for this is that it will affect your tone and things such as how in-depth you might need to go when explaining your subject-matter.

For example, if you're writing for a mature audience that is already familiar with your subject-matter, you may need to back up your statements with references and research, but you may not need to explain terminology you might be using or concepts that are well-understood for the topic.

On the other hand, if you're writing for a very young audience, you might need to go into more depth on definitions and explanations while still making the content fun and engaging.

Just like with exploring aspects of your characters for fiction, take some time to really dig into your ideal reader. You might even do some market research such as interviewing people in your network who would benefit from or be interested in your book and asking them related questions to get an idea of what they'd be looking for or need from the book. You could post questions in Facebook or LinkedIn groups centered around your topic or theme.

Maybe you're writing a book for people going through something in life that you've experienced in order to help them weather that storm. In this case, you could spend some time reflecting on and journaling about your younger self in that time and what you really would've wanted from a book like this during that phase of your life.

Once you have a clear picture of *who* your ideal reader is and what they might be looking for in your book, keep that in mind while you're writing.

Try to picture that reader in your mind as if you're having a conversation in the form of your book. This will make your writing focused and also make your readers feel like you're speaking directly to them.

Again, have fun with it and don't make this something that bogs you down! You don't necessarily have to know every nuance about your ideal reader, but the more specific you can be, the better.

Research

Regardless of if you're writing fiction or non-fiction, research is important.

Different types of research include reading articles that help you learn more about something you're covering but aren't an expert in, other books that elaborate on specific parts of your overall topic and you'd like to include in your writing, material such as graphs, images, or other data that might emphasize or prove a point you're making in non-fiction, or even interviewing experts in areas you'd like to gain more information about for your book.

The most important thing to remember when doing research is not to allow it to become something that inhibits you from completing your book.

One of my clients, before working with me, was in a state of perpetually thinking he needed more and more research before he could even start his book, essentially caught in a fear trap that he was constantly missing one more thing, when in actuality, he had more than enough to create both his first book and an entire backstory!

Also, research can be done throughout the writing process as needed. In my own writing, there have been times I encountered something I needed to research more about only as I was in the middle of writing about it – and I wouldn't have known to do that specific research otherwise!

As you dive into research, give yourself a specific, focused time to do it, write down and save your resources to easily access again, and know exactly what you're researching so you can stay on track and avoid distractions.

If you come across material you think will be useful or relevant, save and include it in your collection of resources, maybe a document of links separate from your notes, and then you can remain focused on your current research topic.

It's good to get as much research as you can done before you start the book, especially for anything you already know you need to learn more about, but again, don't let it become all about the research to the point where you never actually write the book.

Once you've established your pillars for success, you should feel really clear about your book and its direction. Now it's time to write!

Key Takeaways from the Chapter:

- Utilize the four key foundational pillars which are:
  - Your roadmap
  - Your setting
  - Knowing your characters/audience
  - Research

- Always set yourself up for success and you'll accomplish the writing much faster and with much less hurdles to overcome

Chapter 3
Write Your Book

If you've ever tried to finish a book before, you know this is the hardest part. The irony is that for those of you who enjoy writing, it can still feel like such a challenge! However, it doesn't have to be anymore. That's why we spent the last two chapters setting the foundation – and you – up for success.

There are two big rules you need to know as you write your book.

Rule #1: No editing allowed during the first draft.

Rule #2: Keep writing!

No Editing Allowed

While both these rules are pretty straight forward, I want to share with you why they're so important. Writing a book takes time, energy, inspiration, encouragement, and so much more. It's definitely an accomplishment and a commendable feat!

So, during this process, especially as they get further and further into the manuscript, many writers start to lose focus or motivation to continue.

A great way to jumpstart motivation again can be to re-read what you've written in order to get back on track. Many times, from one writing session to the next, a writer might do this to regain their train of thought.

Either way, when reading back through, it can be tempting to make adjustments as you notice things with your fresh pair of eyes, but don't get caught in the editing trap!

If you start trying to edit before the book is done, you'll get bogged down and this book might end up being just another partially-written manuscript gathering dust.

Editing is for the second draft all the way through however many drafts it needs, but until the book is complete, it has no place. That's why there are multiple drafts!

Keep Writing

Another thing that can happen when any loss of motivation or focus strikes is the desire to postpone or put off the book.

Usually, it relates back to one of the causes of writer's block mentioned in chapter one. Most often, this is self-doubt, fear of failure, or even simply disillusionment with the book or thoughts like, "Well, I can always do it later," or "What if no one likes it?" creep in.

This is where being involved in a community or just having a writing buddy can make a huge difference. Even that one other person sharing with you that you're not alone or that they can't wait for your book to be done can help push those thoughts away and keep you going.

Further, you can share with your community or writing buddy an intended deadline for when you'll have your book done. In doing so, this will help you stay focused and on track because instead of giving yourself a goal and then justifying delaying it to yourself, you've now given yourself accountability.

Besides having a buddy and accountability, however, even just for yourself, it's important to keep writing no matter what.

Prove to yourself that you can do it!

Leave yourself notes or write it on your calendar so that you keep pushing toward the completion of your book.

Aside from these rules, I'd like to give you some things you can use to help your actual writing process.

The biggest thing is to commit to writing – and eliminate distractions – during the time you've set aside in your schedule to write. Even if it's just thirty minutes, when you take that time and make it focused and distraction-free, you might be surprised how much progress you can make!

Remember that we as human beings always find time for the important things – like eating and sleeping. So until your book is done, make it a priority. As long as you are setting aside that time, remember that any progress is better than nothing. Just follow the roadmap you've laid out for yourself and keep moving forward.

I want to go back to one of my favorite analogies when it comes to writing, and that is the idea of traveling down a road. As you move further along, things in the distance that might have previously been blurry become clearer. So it is when you're writing your book!

Even with your roadmap, there will still be some areas where you feel less clear about the details of what you'll write or how something might play out. However, as you write your book and get it out of your head and onto the page, it clears up space for your brain to work on the next parts and you'll find that those areas that weren't so clear become more focused. Give it time and let it process, but it will come to you.

However, while your mind is processing these parts, there's a great tool I like to use to come back and fill in the blurry parts later, after they've become clear.

It's bracket writing.

Maybe you've heard of this before and maybe you haven't, but essentially it's putting two brackets into your manuscript, and then inserting a note to yourself about what you'd like to fill in later so you don't forget your train of thought.

It could be merely a descriptive word you can't pinpoint in the moment, or it could be an entire section.

Either way, the goal is to insert these brackets if you're feeling stuck on something, so that you can move on and stay in your zone or flow.

Here's an example from one of my fiction books where I hadn't quite come up with a name for a side-character yet so used brackets (in this case parentheses):

She would let Iolite go and find Amethyst. She had no doubt at the sight of another fae woman of age, Amethyst would rip her to shreds only to later realize she had killed her own long lost daughter and that Iolite had never meant any ill will toward her. A common reaction among fae woman.

The thought of this only made Zyara smile. But that wasn't the extent. She would find Iolite, she was sure of that. But when she did, she would track her and use Iolite to find Amethyst. And then she would finish the bloody wench once and for all.

Fluidly, Zyara turned and stormed out. She rushed once more to main deck. "(Name?)!" she barked, "Change of plans." A smirk slowly formed on her lips. "Get me (runner/spy person Name?)."

(Name(firstmate)?) only nodded and disappeared elsewhere while Zyara headed to her cabin. She moved across the room easily and as soon as she was at her desk grasped some parchment and ink. She began scrawling quickly across the paper, everything beginning to come together. She wrote a letter to each of the fae trafficking ring leaders.

My daughter, Iolite, has finally begun following in my footsteps. She is hunting down our greatest threat, Amethyst, and the Gargoyle. She does so covertly and is pretending to find her to make peace. Should you know of her whereabouts, inform me promptly as she has no way to contact me at the moment.

(Note may change).

This was just the beginning. Soon... Amethyst would be in her clutches.

In using these, I was able to stay in flow and continue making progress, without getting hung-up on minor details. Plus, I could then go back and fill in the gaps later!

The 90 Day Writing Challenge

Okay! You're equipped with the weapons needed to fight writer's block. You've established the pillars for your success, and you have two rules, as well as the tools, needed to write your book.

Yes, there is a lot of pre-work, but all of it will pave the way for your book's completion. Without it, if you try to just dive right in, you'll have just another half-written manuscript set aside, maybe forever!

I now want to present you with the *90 Day Writing Challenge*. This comes from what I've learned over the course of writing my own books.

When you give yourself a deadline, and you share it with friends, family, your accountability buddy, and notes to yourself, all of a sudden, it's not just a 'maybe', a 'someday', or a personal goal. Now, it's a real deadline. Just the same as if you had your own personal agent checking in saying, "What's your progress?" In fact, I encourage you to do this with your accountability buddy!

One of my clients posted sticky notes in the areas of her home where she spent the most time so that she stayed focused on her deadline and that helped her to continuously make progress, even when life got in the way.

Grab your calendar and mark the date 90 days from right now. Circle it in red, add reminders in your phone, maybe even write it in giant letters to yourself on a post-it or a poster board and stick it in your writing place. You can do this!

Remember the creative zone from chapter one? This is the time to commit to tapping into it! Whether that be every day, if your schedule allows, or capitalizing on that time when you can throughout the week, it's important to make it happen consistently.

For now, don't worry about having the right software, beautiful formatting, or anything fancy. This is a first draft, after all!

I used MS Word for *all* of my books. In fact, you can even just use WordPad and then convert it to Word later.

While I believe in a writer following their own inspiration when it comes to writing, whether that be every day or in spurts, think of this as a sprint. You're only committing to writing consistently until your book is complete. That way, it's not extremely overwhelming. Instead, you're working through your roadmap, one step at a time.

As a reminder, you're not alone for this journey, or rather this marathon, of writing a book. To take advantage of being in the private clients-only community and gaining personal guidance and support every step of the way, book your complimentary chat at a convenient time for you:

wewritebooks.com/chat

Bonus Tip: If you're struggling with time to write, you can still get this thing *done* – probably before the 90 days. Use a voice recorder app on your phone and instead of writing, you can dictate your book.

Plus, saying it out loud helps you process in a completely different way, so you may find yourself getting crystal clear on some spots you previously felt stuck getting through. Once you've recorded, you can then get the book transcribed and *voila!*

Key Takeaways from the Chapter:

- No matter how much you do to setup for success, ultimately you must take action and put pen to paper, fingers to keyboard, or record yourself dictating the content

- Always follow the two rules of writing:
  - No editing for the first draft *ever* (done ugly is better than not done at all!)
  - Keep writing and moving forward till you reach *the end.*

- Give yourself a deadline, surround yourself with support for accountability, and *write your book.*

Part II

From Rough Draft
to Reader Ready

Chapter 4
Edits

Wahoo! Congratulations! Whether this is your very first completed book, or you decided to do something different with this one and you just finished, a celebration is in order for you.

Before you dive into edits and all the polishing, take a break and do something fun for yourself. Whether that be going out for a nice dinner, or maybe just getting yourself something you've been wanting, do something to make it truly feel like a celebration.

Also, taking a break – even just a few days – will allow you to look at the book with fresh eyes when you start going back through for edits.

In fact, I even encourage you to put this book aside and then pick it back up to move forward.

Once you've done something to celebrate and taken some time off from your writing, at least for a little bit, it's time to go on to the next part!

Now that you've gotten the book written, everything from here to the finish line is focused on making your book the best it can be and of course, successfully publishing!

In order to help you, I have a free publishing checklist you can use as you go through the process. You can access it inside the *Idea to Print* Bonus Package:

wewritebooks.com/i2pbonus

While during the first draft, there was no editing allowed, now is the time to start the subsequent drafts. There are three phases of edits which are: self-edits, peer-edits, and professional-edits.

Self-Edits

Each of these phases are self-explanatory, but I'll still dive into the details a little. Taking time to comb through the first draft yourself and do self-edits will give you an opportunity to fill in any brackets, catch any plot holes or missing segments, and start to tighten up the writing.

I recommend reading out loud to yourself. When you're reading out loud instead of just in your head, more senses are engaged which means you'll hear and catch more mistakes.

Also, since you're the one who wrote the book, if you're reading silently, there may be areas where your brain automatically connects the dots if something isn't quite detailed enough or you overlook small mistakes because you know what you're trying to say.

Even if you can't speak at normal volume, just whispering the words will have the same result.

Go through the book at least once yourself, but if you can, go through again after the first edits to make sure that everything is flowing and there aren't immediate mistakes jumping out at you.

Peer-Edits

Once you've gone through yourself, it's time to engage those friends and family-members who have been eagerly awaiting the completion of your book. These are your beta-readers – essentially readers that give you feedback on the book in exchange for early access to your wonderful writing. These can also be fellow writers and many authors "exchange" beta-readings with each other.

I want to take a brief moment to share with you that while peer-edits can be a great resource for helping to gain reader insights and even making it more polished before sending it to the editor, it's also something you can do *after* the professional edits or even to use as a last stretch of feedback before the launch.

If you do choose to have peer-edits before sending to the editor, I recommend having at least one or two beta-readers that are fellow writers, as they understand both the writer's and reader's perspective, and can therefore offer you feedback about the story while still respecting your voice as the author.

Take feedback at this stage with a grain of salt. You'll get mixed feedback from different people, since others will have their own ideas or opinions. Look for the feedback that is consistent and don't be afraid to reject feedback based on what you think works best for the story or characters. After all, you know it best!

Finally, ask your beta readers if they will be a part of your launch team, when the time comes, to give the book an honest review once it's published. It's important to get as much support for the book as you can!

Professional Edits

I've heard the argument many times about whether or not a professional editor is really necessary. I learned the hard way that, yes, it is.

When I was starting out, I was very excited about my first book. I landed a publishing deal and thought that everything was going to be all sunshine and roses.

Instead, I found out only after signing the contract that my publisher did *not* offer editing services. In fact, the publishing agent only gave me a few suggestions and then left the edits to me.

At the time, I was still very naïve when it came to the publishing industry and I thought, "Well I'm pretty good at writing and pretty good at grammar, editing, and proofreading. I'm sure I can just do it myself and I'll be fine."

I got a couple of friends to look it over, but they didn't want to hurt my feelings and they didn't have the experience of the industry to tell me the critical feedback I actually *needed*.

So, very gung ho and certain my book would be great, I resubmitted to the publisher. They were happy with the changes after looking over the first couple of chapters, so moved forward with publishing the book.

Once it was released, it was to my absolute dismay that I only then began to notice tons of mistakes. Not to mention I started getting feedback from readers about what should've been changed.

I was horrified and scrambled to work with the publisher for a second edition release. However, by that point, it was too late. My initial reputation and the book's were soured. One review said, "I'm not sure if I'd read anything else by this author." I wanted to cry.

After that, I determined to never again release a book without having a professional editor look it over. What I've learned about having a professional is that they can not only provide unbiased, critical but necessary feedback, but they also have experience with a wide variety of works in the industry and can tell you exactly what readers will be looking for.

When you find the right editor for you, that editor will often become your editor for life. They will respect your unique author voice, while still making the book the absolute best it can be.

As you start looking for a professional, first reach out to your writing community and your social sphere. Maybe someone you know has a referral or a fellow author can give you a suggestion.

Often, by doing so, you'll be able to work with someone not only recommended, but someone that can work with your budget.

If you're having no luck in your community, look on Fiverr or Upwork for a freelance editor. Make sure you do your research before making a hire. You'll want someone that has experience and good reviews, offers the type of editing you're looking for, whether that be full edits or just proofreading, and can pay attention to you and your work.

Further, be specific in your request to help you weed out the people who are just applying for everything they can. You can even include a brief extract of your book and request a sample edit to make sure you two will be a good fit.

One thing I love about Upwork is that you can include specific questions you'd like applicants to answer in your request for submissions, almost like a pre-interview!

I've included one of the postings I made for one of my fiction novels below, as well as some suggestions for when you make your own!

My posting:

I am looking for someone to critically review and edit my novel. It is 68k words for now. The plot is set in a world heavily based off of the Golden Age of Sail in the 17th century and centers around pirates and one fae-woman's struggle. I will need feedback on the flow, the structure overall, the feel, the consistency, and whether everything ties together in a way that makes sense.

Hours to be determined	Less than 1 month	Intermediate level
Hourly	Project Length	$$ I am looking for a mix of experience and value

Attachment
RTP Chapter 1.docx (25 KB)

You will be asked to answer the following questions when submitting a proposal:
1. What is your experience with editing? Fiction or non-fiction or both? What are your tastes when you select leisure reading? Where are you from? What is your typical availability?

Skills and expertise

Editing

It was simple but to the point, and asking the questions helped me to find exactly what I was looking for – and also gave applying editors an idea of what to expect from me.

When you're writing your own posting, you can also request that applicants include a specific statement in

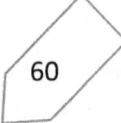

their submission, such as "I love editing" or something odd and random like "flying squirrels", so that you can truly see who's paying attention to everything you've written!

As you're interviewing potential editors, trust your instincts. If something feels 'off', even if you can't quite explain it, go with someone else.

One important note to make is that when you work with me and my team, you receive access to highly recommended, vetted professionals including comprehensive editors. When you choose the coaching package, these services are provided for you as part of the package so you can know with confidence your book is the best it can be. To discuss taking advantage of this, choose a convenient time to chat here:

wewritebooks.com/chat

Once you've hired your editor, I recommend going back and forth with the manuscript three times over the course of three to four weeks. This process will allow the editor a chance to truly go through with a fine-toothed comb.

If it's a full edit, maybe the first round can be tackling things like flow, structure, and development and then the second round can tackle proofreading for grammar, sentence structure, and punctuation. Finally, the third round is to give all the edits and changes a final look from a little bit of a step back to give you feedback on everything as a whole.

Once your book has been approved by the editor, it should be polished, shiny, and ready to make its appearance in the world. Now there are just a few steps in between to really make sure it starts its published life with a bang!

Key Takeaways from the Chapter:

- As you begin self-edits, read the book out loud, even whispered, to yourself.

- Getting a professional editor is *always* a worthy investment in the success of your book. If you're going to cut corners, don't cut this one.

- For any beta-readers who get involved, ask if they'll support your book launch. You can also offer an exchange and support them!

Chapter 5
Your Cover

This is one of my favorite parts of the process. There's something magical and final about seeing the completed cover of your book for the first time – and even more so when it arrives in the mail as part of your printed and bound book!

Just like with editing, your cover is not something I recommend doing yourself, unless you are excellent with photoshop and can make it look professional.

Opposite to the common saying, "Don't judge a book by its cover," that's exactly what readers do the first time they cross paths with your book. It doesn't have to be elaborate. In fact, sometimes the simplest of covers lead to the most sales. The important thing is that it grabs attention, creates intrigue, and looks professional.

Also, it doesn't need to break the bank either. First, ask around in your community if anyone would recommend a cover designer. This doesn't have to be only in your writing community. Maybe you've got a friend or someone you know that is a master of graphic design and would love the opportunity to have their work featured front and center on your book.

If not, you can look on Upwork or Fiverr, just like with the editor, for someone that does cover designs and fits within your budget. This also allows you to look at their previous work, find a style you like, and verify that you'll get great work.

Bonus Tip: If you're writing a children's book, and you aren't doing the art yourself, you can also find your illustrator in the same way.

There are three major components of a cover that you'll need to consider before submitting to your designer or making your cover (if you're doing it yourself). These include: the design, the blurb, and, of course, your name and title.

Design

If you haven't already, you'll need to brainstorm some ideas of how you want your cover to look. You can research other books in your genre, or simply consider images and colors that relate to your story or content.

As you're looking at similar books, take note of what colors they have. Choosing something different will help your book to stand out and pop out of the page among the myriad of other options.

For example, if you notice that other books in the genre have lots of blues or cooler colors, you could choose orange, red, or another warmer color.

For images, remember there's a difference between a book that looks pretty and a book that sells.

What I mean by this is that sometimes, if a cover is a gorgeous piece of art, but it has too much going on at once, it might feel overwhelming or confusing to the prospective reader, instead of creating the curiosity and intrigue that the cover should be creating. I'm in no way saying the cover shouldn't look amazing, but just be aware of how much is going on at once.

With the design, the text for the title and your name can also play a factor, so we'll go into this in the name and title section.

For example, consider the Game of Thrones original book covers, or if you're writing non-fiction, scroll through some business books on Amazon, and you'll see that many of them have a singular image, if any at all.

They primarily focus on large text and colors that stand out and demand your attention. Even covers that have full backgrounds have a focal point or primary image.

Here are some examples of both fiction and non-fiction from the top 100 sellers on Amazon:

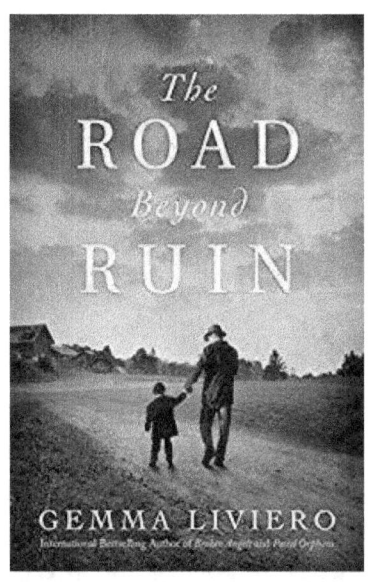

As you're considering the design you want for your cover, the most important thing is to have fun with it and not to get too overwhelmed. Especially if you're entrusting the design to a chosen designer, all you have to do is give them an idea of what you're going for, and leave the outcome to their capable, experienced hands.

Blurb

The book blurb is just as important as the cover design when it comes to drawing your prospective reader in and creating enough curiosity and intrigue for them to want to buy your book.

If it's fiction, the goal is to give the reader an idea of the plot without giving everything away. If it's non-fiction, the goal is to make the reader feel like they'll gain something or solve a problem they have by reading your book.

Before tackling your blurb, take a bit of time to do some research. Read the blurbs of the top ten selling books in your genre, or read the blurb from some of your favorite movies or T.V. shows in that genre. What about these blurbs draws you in?

Get some feedback from your writing community or your writing buddy. Others can offer you the outside perspective of a potential buyer of your book, plus you may find that a fellow writer can give you some suggestions on how to make your blurb really shine.

Once you submit your blurb, you can also ask your cover designer for his or her feedback, since your designer will have experience with other blurbs and can also give you some valuable insight.

Also, remember that it doesn't have to be final. You can always change or update it later if you feel you need to!

Your Author Name and Book Title

It's time to make the official decision, if you haven't already. Will you be using your name, or a pen name? And what will the title of your book be?

Ultimately, whether you use your name or a pen name, this decision is up to you. No one else can make it for you. In my experience, this is usually something personal and also meaningful to you.

For example, for my fiction books, I chose to use a pen name because I knew I wanted to write non-fiction as well and wanted to have that differentiation. When I chose the name itself, it related back to how I feel connected to my mom through my writing, so it means a lot to me, even if no one else understands.

For your title, I'll share that titles are especially difficult for me, though maybe for you they're a piece of cake.

With fiction, a title can be more fun, mysterious, and may or may not actually have anything to do with the book.

For example, I never understood what 'Twilight' had to do with the actual story. Of course, there's speculation – but in the end I couldn't figure it out. Even the author has admitted that the title "isn't perfect". Nevertheless, you could choose something like this, but I still recommend choosing a fiction title that includes something within the book.

With non-fiction, the title needs to be more specific as well as direct and clear to your ideal reader. If you try to be mysterious with a non-fiction title, you'll find that prospective readers are confused, instead of curious, and usually won't buy. Tell them what your book can offer them or what problem it will solve.

Whether fiction or non-fiction, if you do struggle with titles, brainstorm some ideas and then ask your community for some votes.

This is also a great way to start gathering curiosity and interest around your book to build momentum for when

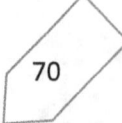

it's time to publish. In fact, you might even get a suggestion from someone that you fall in love with. How cool for that reader to have their suggestion be the title of the book? I bet they will become a fan!

Now that you have your name and title, it's time to include them in the cover submission to your designer. One of the mistakes I made with my first book was that I squished my author name and book title together and it made the cover feel like too much. A lesson I learned was to space out the name and title so that they're distinguished all on their own.

Don't be afraid to have your name in big letters, either. Be proud of the fact that your name is officially on a book! If you're doing your own cover, make sure you choose fonts that are easy to read and also colors which contrast but don't look faded.

One of the biggest things that scream non-professional on a cover is a poor choice of fonts and colors when it comes to the text. If your designer sends you something that looks 'off', don't be afraid to ask for changes.

Your cover is your reader's first impression.

Finally, something I recommend is asking your designer for two slightly different covers. Maybe they use differing colors or integrate two different images.

The reason is that, just like with choosing your title, you can showcase the covers on social media and get feedback on which others like best. This not only gives you an idea of how prospective readers will respond once you're published, but also helps to gather more interest for your upcoming book release.

As I shared for the editor, this also encompasses a cover designer should you choose to work with me and my team. If you'd like to work with one of our designers, reach out and let's chat:

wewritebooks.com/chat

If you're in love with the cover and only want one design, you can also do an online cover reveal and make it a party, perhaps with a lucky competition winner getting a free copy (once the book is published), or just use it as a chance to ask for thoughts on your exciting reveal.

Share your cover in as many places as possible – writing communities, your personal or author (if using a pen name) Facebook page, even to your coworkers, friends, and family by pulling up the image on your phone.

Most of all, continue to have fun with it and truly make it a celebration.

Key Takeaways from the Chapter:

- A cover is a first impression. It needs to stand out, grab attention, and draw the reader in.

- Announcing your cover is a great way to start getting support and interest for your upcoming book launch.

Chapter 6
Formatting

When I mention formatting, I'm going to discuss both the actual internal design of the book as well as the types of formats you can offer to potential readers.

As I mentioned previously, I use MS Word for all of my books, including the internal design. Word is versatile because you can choose your page margins, book size (for print), fonts, and everything else.

The main formats in today's industry include eBook, print, and audiobook. For print and eBook, you'll have slightly different internal designs, so I recommend saving separate files of your book for each one.

An eBook does not have to have page numbers and you'll want to be careful when adding boxes or images, as they'll look different across a variety of reading devices.

For eBooks, it's best to leave the design as simple as possible. Definitely include page breaks and spacing, but don't get too caught up in the design itself.

Another thing to consider for eBooks is paragraph length. Depending on your page size, print allows for slightly longer paragraphs, but on an e-reader device, which is often hand-held, like a phone, long paragraphs can feel overwhelming to the reader and cause them to skim over parts of your book or decide not to finish it at all.

Unlike the eBook, a print book will look exactly how you design it. In fact, when self-publishing, on-demand printers often provide a book previewer so that you can make sure your print book really does look the way you want it to.

Your print version is where you can truly dig into the fun of designing your book's pages. If you're writing fiction, you can play with fun images on your chapters' first letters or titles. With non-fiction, you can include boxes with quotes or pieces of content you want to draw extra attention to. For both, you want to include page numbers and maybe even chapter titles on each page.

While you're formatting, this is also an excellent time to add in any additional pages such as your title page, table of contents, acknowledgements, copyright page, and 'about the author' page.

Standard print sizes are usually 5x8 or 6x9 and you'll want to make sure your margins are appropriate so it doesn't look like your text is squished on the page. Word actually offers a 'mirrored' margins option specifically for print books, which you can then customize further.

The most important thing for paperback formatting is to go through carefully and make sure everything looks the way you want it to, such as including all the necessary pages, spacing between paragraphs, indents, images, and chapter titles, before you add in the page numbers and any other headers and footers. The reason for this is that unlike with eBook, which needs to be flexible across multiple devices and thus has more freedom for movement, paperback will turn out exactly the way it is on the page, and one small change can affect the text elsewhere.

Once you've finished the paperback formats, it's important to save it in PDF. Anytime you're uploading for publication and printing, these services require paperback files to be in PDF (which also includes the cover). This way, it's print ready and there is much less room for error. You can then feel confident your finished product will turn out just the way you envision it.

As an additional note, if you prefer *not* to use MS Word, Reedsy offers book formatting or, if you use Mac, Vellum is a great formatting tool. Furthermore, if you'd rather not mess with formatting at all, you can outsource it. You could ask in your favorite writing community for recommendations, or look for someone on Upwork or Fiverr.

Finally, as with the editing and cover design, when you work with me and my team, there is support as well as formatting services available so you have as few things to worry about as possible through each part of the process. Remember, you're never alone! Chat with me about working together here:

wewritebooks.com/chat

For audiobooks, don't feel overwhelmed or pressured to have that done by the time the book is published, unless you really want to. Audiobooks are a great way to reach an additional audience, but if you have an eBook and a print version, you're absolutely ready to go. When you are ready to complete the audiobook, you can choose to record yourself or hire someone else to do it for you.

Amazon offers services to help you turn your book into an audiobook, and you can also hire a freelancer. In fact, you may even have a friend that would enjoy doing a recording reading your book.

The biggest thing to consider, if you do it yourself or have a friend do it, is that the recording needs to sound clean and professional. That means no background noise or static, and the recording itself needs to be clear.

You can use a recording app on your phone such as Rev, and then upload to your computer, or you could also simply record on your computer with a good microphone and a program like Audacity.

From there, you can choose to upload it to your distributor, such as Amazon, or even make it a special separate purchase or download for your readers. We'll get into details of uploading in upcoming chapters.

One last thing to note on formatting is that you don't want to release all the possible formats at once. Not only will it allow you to focus on one thing at a time, meaning less overwhelm and a smoother release, but it also means that you can keep excitement and momentum going for your book after it's been published.

Maybe you release the print version a few weeks after the eBook comes out and then the audiobook several weeks after that. You could even do the audiobook as a special anniversary release a year after your book is published.

Bonus Tip: If you decide to have your book available on your website in any capacity, or from other sources than the distributors (such as Amazon, IngramSpark, etc.), use Calibre. This is a book conversion software which has a broad range of capabilities for converting books and is quite user friendly. It's free to download and allows you to offer your book to your readers in their favorite format.

Whatever you decide, you can use the release of new formats as a way to continue celebrating your book with your community and talking about it long after the official publication date. After all, who says the party has to stop?

Key Takeaways from the Chapter:

- Formatting is largely about what you personally like to see in a book, aesthetically – so have fun with it!

- Save a separate file for eBook and Paperback when formatting.

- EBook needs to be flexible across many reading devices while paperback will look *exactly* as is so requires more attention to detail.

Chapter 7
Final Pieces

You're almost ready to send your book out into the world and into readers' hands. Now that the book is polished, formatted, and has a great cover, there are just a couple of things I recommend before you start the homestretch to publication.

Whether you're writing fiction or non-fiction, take a step back and revisit your reasons for writing this book. What was your purpose? Was it to pursue your dream of creating a career as an author and going on to publish many more? Or to either start a business through your book or reach a larger audience for your current business?

Part of achieving these goals is establishing and growing your reader audience.

Even before your book is published, it's important to be able to gather your readers into one place where you can reach them about new releases, exciting updates, or other news from you as an author. By doing so, you'll exponentially increase your results with each new book you release in the future. If your goals are more business-focused, think of this as more like growing your potential customer base.

You've already started growing interest in your book by sharing your cover and getting input, but before you announce your official upcoming release, it's important to make sure you're set up for success behind the scenes so that you can truly relax and enjoy the celebration when it's time to announce your book is live.

You're probably already familiar with what an email list is, but if you don't already have one, now is the time!

This is exactly what I was talking about when I mentioned having one place where you can gather your readers. Not only will you know which readers truly are your fans, but you'll have an opportunity to build an even stronger author-reader relationship with them by communicating with them regularly – even once or twice a month works well.

There are several great email list management websites to get you started, like MailChimp, which is free to use for up to 2,000 subscribers. Once you create your account, spend some time familiarizing yourself with the forms and email types so that you feel more comfortable and not overwhelmed.

You can create a signup form for your website, set up an automated email for when new readers sign up for your list, and link your social media accounts in the emails so that readers have more places to follow you.

If you're using a pen name, or even if you're using your name but haven't set up social media pages specifically for your authorship, now is a great time to do so.

You don't have to set something up on every platform out there. Start with your favorite one or two you feel most comfortable with and then, if you decide you'd like to have something on other platforms, you can do so later.

Finally, now is a great time to consider having your own website. Just like with your cover, simplicity can work well!

In fact, to start out, you could just have a singular page inviting your readers to sign up for your list in exchange for a free copy of your eBook, or maybe another work you'd like to offer instead, such as an unrelated short story, the back-story to your book, or if it's non-fiction, a helpful guide related to your book.

Once the new reader subscribes to your list, you can include the freebie in the form of a link or a downloadable file in the welcome email you set up in your email list provider.

It doesn't have to be expensive either! Wix offers free website services, or if you prefer WordPress, you can purchase a domain name from DreamHost and link it to WordPress with hosting for less than $10 a month. Over time, you can expand your website as much as you like or leave it simple.

In addition to the signup page, you could have a home page that features your book and some info about you as the author. Having a home page is also a great place to add a form for readers to sign up for your list. WordPress and Wix both offer easy-to-use plugins for many email list providers so that you don't even have to mess with code, unless you want to.

For some inspiration, check out the websites of other authors in your genre or your favorite authors. If you're just doing the signup page for now, it can be full of color and design or super simple. Maybe it just has a cool design and a form for their name and email address. Make it feel like *you*.

Finally, don't forget to include your signup page on your social media sites!

As a part of working with me and my team, we guide you step-by-step through every part of this process, including tutorials, trainings, templates, and top recommended tools of the trade. (Try saying those five times fast!) That way, there is little guesswork. Instead, there is confident implementation, knowing you're setup for success for this book, as well as any future books you pursue. To partner with me or learn more about gaining support, book a time to chat:

wewritebooks.com/chat

Once you've set up your email list, including an email that welcomes new subscribers, created your social media pages, and your website page or pages are live, you're ready to start the homestretch to publication.

You've done a ton of legwork, so now it's time to prepare for the celebration. Seriously, take a moment to look back on how much you've accomplished so far! I, for one, can't wait to see your creation in print.

Key Takeaways from the Chapter:

- Before you start the pre-launch and book launch, it's important to prepare your website and email database. It can be simple but should encourage your readers to continue engaging with you and your book.

* Include a simple sequence to invite new subscribers to read your book and leave a review.

Part III

The Road to Publication

Chapter 8
Building Momentum and Your Reader Community

With all of the backend work done, now is a great time to go ahead and set your publication date. I recommend giving yourself at least a few weeks from now so you have plenty of time to get set up with your distributor and make sure everything goes smoothly.

Once you've selected your date, announce it to the world. Share it on social media, add a headline to your website, share in your writing community, tell all your friends and family. In fact, feel free to shoot me an email at *katelyn@wewritebooks.com* and share your upcoming release date with me! I'd love to check out your book.

As you're sharing details of your upcoming book launch, this is the perfect opportunity to invite potential readers to sign up for your list. Don't ask them by saying, "Sign up for my list."

Instead, entice them, just like with your book blurb, by offering them a *reason* to sign up, such as a freebie they'll receive as well as immediate updates as the book nears release and once publication day arrives.

Another great opportunity while you're sharing your release date is to start asking who would be interested in helping you with the book launch.

You may or may not have already heard of a book launch team, but in essence, it's a group of people that rally behind your book to help it have the best possible chance of success from the get-go.

These might be fellow authors who aren't quite ready to publish and would be interested in seeing how you go about it. It could also be fans who believe in you or your book and just want to be a part. Don't disregard anyone!

When you're asking, share that in exchange for a free first-look at the book before release, you're looking for some people to form a launch team which includes downloading and leaving an *honest* review of the book during the first week of launch. (You definitely don't want people to feel like they have to lie or that you're trying to get false reviews). Make sure they know what they're signing up for. If they can't commit to that, it's okay to say no.

Your goal is to get at least fifteen to twenty people on your team. The reason behind this is not only will it hugely help your initial momentum for the book launch, but once you have more than ten reviews, you can start submitting your book to promotion websites to reach an even wider audience.

Realistically speaking, you won't get 100% of the people on your team to follow through. People get busy, they forget, and things come up, but try to get there with as many as possible.

Note: there are different book launch strategies discussed in chapter ten, some of which fit perfectly with having a launch team, and others which don't require one.

I recommend reading through these strategies to decide which approach will work best for you and then choosing if you'd like to have a launch team or not.

If not, it's still fantastic to share your upcoming date, though instead of asking who would be interested in seeing behind the scenes, you'll just focus on building excitement.

Once you've gotten their interest, at the bare minimum, ask your launch team members for their email address.

You can add them to your email list in a segment or special group specifically for the book launch and then email them their free copy of the book as well as updates and what to expect as you get closer to launch. You can also email them on launch day to let them know the book is out and once again ask them to download and review it.

I recommend creating a private Facebook group where you can invite the members of your team to join together. This allows them to see who else is on the team, communicate, and also it can serve as an extra motivator if some members are behind but see that other members have already read the book.

It makes updates from you quick and easy, you can upload their free copy of the book in the files, and it also makes it hassle-free for them to give you any last-minute feedback before the book is published.

Within your group, you can "go live" to talk about your book, your journey, and thank everyone for being there. Or, if you're not comfortable in front of the camera, you can simply post in the group so everyone knows what's going on and what to expect.

You can also ask your group members to share the news on their own social media accounts once the book is released, so that you reach not just your immediate community, but theirs too.

As you can see, once you set a publication date and start sharing with the world, there are tons of ways to start creating interest and support for your book before it's even released.

Each week, continue talking about the upcoming release until the big day. It can be a quick post, a video, or anything you love doing and feel great about, as long as it keeps the excitement and energy for the book going. Plus it doesn't let anyone forget about it! You could even do a count-down as you near the official date with a daily post of how many days are left. Get creative and have fun with it.

Key Takeaways from the Chapter:

- Once all the pieces are in place, choose your launch date and announce it to the world.

* Start inviting supporters to help launch the book; be clear about expectations and make sure only those truly invested in helping you succeed are joining in.

Chapter 9
Setting Up Your Book Release to Go Off with a Bang

As you probably know, there are lots of options when it comes to publishing, such as Amazon, IngramSpark, Lulu, Barnes & Noble, Smashwords, and Kobo. At least to start off, I recommend going with Amazon and here's why.

While there is definitely tons of competition, think of it in terms of your reach and opportunity. I've personally opted for a variety of book formats including ePub and PDF, which are the two outside of the .mobi files used for Kindle, and I will say that as far as hassle, simply getting the book via Amazon straight to my phone's Kindle app is the easiest and most direct method.

(If you choose to publish outside of Amazon, having an ePub is what you'll need for Nook users.)

> **Bonus Tip:** For easy file conversions to different formats, Amazon also offers Kindle Create, a free program that will convert to any format you need.

In today's world, where many people are busy and want things as easily and simply as possible, starting with Amazon for your book makes things easier for your readers. Also, because Amazon is so large, it literally has instant reach to millions of potential readers.

Your job is to set your book up for success so that it is the one readers choose ahead of your competition.

Of course, once your book launch is over, you can explore other platforms if you want, or even play with adding an option for readers to buy your book directly from your website.

For now, let's focus on getting your book set up and published through Amazon. When uploading to Amazon, you don't need to convert your file. Simply .doc or .docx, both MS Word formats, will work and Amazon will complete the conversion for you.

You already have a great, attention-grabbing cover, an intrigue-building blurb, and a team to support your launch, so now it's just bringing it together.

At least one week before your announced launch date, go ahead and get your book uploaded. This gives you time to familiarize yourself with the Amazon KDP area and setup, work through all aspects of setting up your book, and make sure you catch any bugs or kinks before it's official.

I wouldn't recommend setting your book up as a pre-release as this doesn't actually help your initial momentum. Go ahead and hit 'publish'!

I want to take a brief moment to share about some different strategies through this process. There are some methods which advocate for publishing your book elsewhere, such as iBooks, sending lots of readers via promotion or through large group collaborations, and then launching through Amazon afterward.

It's been my experience that doing so requires an existing audience of readers or a large, specific marketing budget. I think that doing author collaboration is extremely valuable also, however, for the purpose of this book, my focus is guiding you through the process primarily if this is your first book. Everything I'm sharing with you is tried and true, not only for my books, but those of numerous clients. These methods will allow you to get in front of readers and start growing your audience.

Once you've built your audience, you will see a snowball effect for future books, or if you're in business, then new clientele and opportunities. As you grow and build traction, you can reinvest that in your book or in future books.

It's always a great idea to start getting eyeballs and readers to your book page as quickly as possible once the book is 'live'. Therefore, I don't recommend uploading more than those few days in advance so you can still take advantage of the 'new release' time frame. For Amazon, it's the first thirty days after a book is published.

Ideally, the optimal is to start bringing readers to the page on day one. Uploading a few days in advance allows you to give plenty of breathing room before you're announcing it, in case you need to make any last-minute adjustments. However, as soon as you receive notice from Amazon that your book is ready to go, and you've reviewed it and are happy with the result, you're welcome to start privately letting your launch team or anyone supporting you know to go ahead and download the book.

Don't forget to be the first 'purchase' for your book once it's live!

Part of the upload process includes setting a book price. We'll talk about pricing strategies in the next chapter, but for now, go ahead and pick something you feel comfortable with until the official launch.

During your set up, you'll have an opportunity to choose your book's categories. Did you know Amazon allows you to choose up to ten categories for your book? In this initial set up, you'll only see space for two, but afterwards, you can email support to request additional categories.

As you're choosing and considering categories, there are tons of great ways to make sure you leverage your categories to further help your book release.

You've probably heard of KDP Rocket, which does research for you and gives you suggestions. There are also some freelancers that provide category assistance services for low cost. You can also ask your writing community for recommendations. However, I'm going to share how you can do your own research as well.

If you go into the main Kindle books area on Amazon, on the left-hand side you'll see a list of all the main categories. Within those are subcategories.

Grab a paper and pen and, of the main categories, write down any your book could fall into. Afterwards, click into those categories and for each one, note the subcategories most appropriate. Continue until you've reached the smallest level.

As you're going into each category, also take a moment to note the top book in each. Click into that book and about halfway down the page you'll be able to see that book's ranking in its top three categories as well as its overall Amazon ranking.

Focus on the overall ranking and, if the book is ranked better than 20,000th overall, know that its top categories will be highly competitive and thus more difficult for you to achieve higher rankings, unless you've already got a large audience anticipating your book.

However, if you notice that the top book's overall ranking is between 70,000th and 300,000th, these categories will allow you to achieve a high rank within the smaller categories with less competition, and you'll also have an easier time sustaining that ranking.

If the book is ranked closer to the 500,000th mark and above, these categories probably don't have a lot of interest and probably aren't great choices for your book.

The idea is to choose subcategories which you can rank highly in, creating more visibility and opportunity for your book long term, while still getting exposure to a wide audience.

If you stay highly ranked in smaller categories, you can then aim for higher ranks in larger categories. Plus, by aiming high in smaller categories, you have a higher chance of attaining the orange bestseller banner, and that's something you can use for life!

Bonus Tip: While you're doing this research, you can also take note of prices for competing books in your selected categories.

We'll talk about pricing strategy in the next chapter, but pricing a little lower on your book after the launch phase can help drive sales toward your book versus your competitors, and may even strike up some friendly competition.

Once you've selected your categories, submit them to KDP support to give your book maximum visibility among Amazon book shoppers.

After you've verified everything is ready to go, it's time to share with your launch team and start getting ready for launch day! You can go ahead and prepare some social media posts as well and ask your team to share them in turn.

If all of this seems like a lot, I want to put your mind at ease and encourage you to take it one step at a time. Read through the next chapter to decide on a winning book launch strategy. Then, make a clear, intentional plan of execution, each day or week until launch.

One of the most important factors for me during my first book launches was having guidance in the form of a mentor every step of the way through the process. It made such a world of difference.

If you'd like to have that same personal support through the process, I'd love to not only celebrate your huge accomplishment, but help you in implementation. Let's chat about working together on your exciting book launch:

wewritebooks.com/chat

Key Takeaways from the Chapter:

- A few days before the official launch day, go ahead and get your book uploaded and hit 'publish'.

- Select up to ten categories for your book and send a support request to Amazon so your book has as much visibility as possible.

- Start getting readers on the book page as soon as possible once everything is ready to go.

Chapter 10
Launch Your Book and Your Career

Woohoo! It's time for your launch week! Are you ready?

In this chapter, I want to go over a few different launch strategies I've learned about and personally tried or participated in, to help you as you release your book to the world.

This list doesn't comprehensively cover all of the strategies that exist for a book launch, but they do all work and have their own pros and cons to consider.

Also, these are great strategies for helping build support for your book whether you have a large following of readers or not. These include the free strategy and the

99¢ strategy for pricing, as well as the author takeover strategy and the traditional approach for growing interest in your book.

One other amazing strategy is the book funnel strategy. For this book, I won't be going into tons of detail on it, however, I've included a very in-depth resource to learn more and implement this strategy if you choose to do so.

One last thing before we dive into the strategies is not to let yourself get too overwhelmed. Remember that with so much going on, mistakes or technical errors can happen!

In fact, I don't think I've ever had a launch where at least one thing didn't go wrong. That's why we took the time to set up as much as possible beforehand, but the most important thing to remember is that if something does go wrong, don't let it take you out.

Instead, attack it head on with a "can do anything" attitude, make adjustments, and keep going!

Perseverance leads to success much more than everything going perfectly with no errors – both with your book and with many things in life.

So embrace the process and focus on the wins. After all, you're publishing your book!

The Free Strategy

This strategy is really great for anyone with no audience, although it can still be used if you have one as a cool way to thank your fans.

Since your book has already been uploaded and tested for any kinks prior to launch, this strategy is all about playing with numbers and getting as many downloads as possible. You could even make it a game!

One to two days before your launch day, go into the KDP dashboard and set up a promotion for your book to be listed as free. Amazon gives you up to five promotional days per quarter, so you can choose to use all five or maybe just three for now.

In fact, if you choose five but only announce the book will be free for three days, and then things are going well, you can later announce a surprise extension for the remaining two days. Otherwise, you can simply end the promotion in the dashboard after three days and choose the remaining two at another time. The system is flexible so make the most of it.

Once you're notified by Amazon that the promotion has started, it's time to go live!

Now is the time to party and celebrate. First, let your launch team know the promotion has started and ask them to download and leave their review. This does two important things.

One, it gives you a huge boost in Amazon ranking because your book will start getting lots of attention as it's downloaded and reviewed. The reviews don't all have to be five stars, and you should encourage your team members to be honest. However, this is where it all comes together and really gives your book an explosive launch.

As the book starts getting attention, Amazon will start featuring your book in Hot New Release areas for its categories, which will give it even more views and downloads from Amazon shoppers.

Two, ensuring they download the book verifies all of your team members' reviews so that each one shows up as an 'Amazon Verified Review' and is legitimate according to Amazon's algorithms.

After your launch team, post on social media, share with friends and family – shout it to the world! You're published! And it's free for a limited time!

Also, this is a perfect time to start asking your launch team to share the news that your book is live on their social media as well.

Bonus Tip: When you're sharing the link, instead of just grabbing the web address from the address bar from a search, follow these steps to get a clean link:

1. Go to your Amazon dashboard Bookshelf.
2. Scroll to the book area on the page.
3. If you're on a computer, hover over the link: "View on Amazon".
4. If on a mobile device, tap on the link: "View on Amazon".
5. Click or tap on your country.
6. Copy the link from the address bar on the page that opens.

See below for provided example:

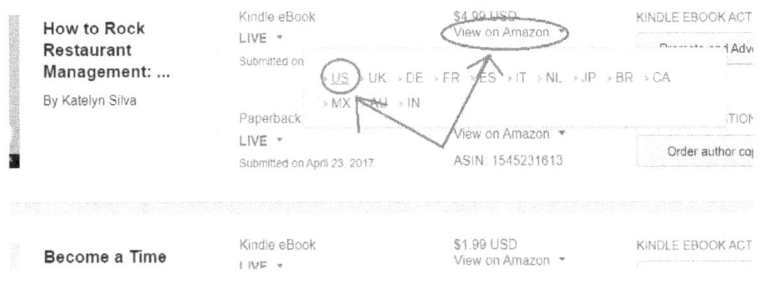

Grab the link from the address bar in the page that opens as it's a clean, direct link without any search tags or anything else.

The trick for sustaining the momentum you've gathered with the Free Strategy is timing. What I mean by this is that you want to be in control of when your promotion ends, instead of letting Amazon just finish it at midnight.

The majority of books aren't being sold at midnight, after all.

When are they being sold?

Typically between about 3pm and 8pm, give or take depending on time zone, right? For a US audience, in order to account for as many people between Eastern and Pacific as possible, I suggest 3pm Central as the time to manually end the promotion in your dashboard.

On the day before your promotion ends, adjust the listed price to 99¢ so that when the promotion ends, the book will be listed at that price.

Then, on the last day of the promotion, click the "End Promotion" button around 3pm Central Time. What happens is Amazon takes time to catch up and process the change, but in the meantime, your book will still be listed in the free store where it's gained all that momentum and ranking. However, it will now be listed at the 99¢ mark.

Many people viewing the book will think, "Well 99¢ is basically free anyway," and will still buy it. Then, when Amazon catches up with the promotion ending, all those downloads at 99¢ will count as purchases that boost your ranking in the paid store.

Keep an eye on your KDP dashboard during this time and keep talking about your book as much as you can! Share pictures of milestones and changes in ranking, especially if you get #1 in your categories, are featured on the Hot New Release areas, or reach download milestones like 100, 500, 1000... your launch team and others will want to know and celebrate with you!

Once the free period is over, share that your book is being listed at 99¢. This is a great time to build further momentum by featuring the book on book promotion sites now that it has all those reviews and has enjoyed that boost in ranking.

You might choose to leave it at 99¢ for a day, or even a couple weeks. When pricing, Amazon provides a graph showing optimum price based on similar books and book length. You can choose to simply jump to that price after the 99¢ period, or slowly climb in $1 increments to see how it affects your downloads to find the sweet spot for your book.

Again, this strategy is all about numbers and timing, so you always want to plan accordingly ahead of time for your big days of announcement and changes. It's also a fantastic strategy if you've got little to no audience, because who can resist a free book?

The 99¢ Strategy

This strategy is somewhat similar to the Free Strategy but it doesn't have a focus on timing. Again, the goal is gathering tons of downloads and attention for the book in the first days of launch, and it also factors in the psychology that 99¢ is basically free.

Just like with the free strategy, one to two days before the launch day, go ahead and set up a promotion in the KDP dashboard, but instead of listing as free, choose 99¢ as the promotion price.

Bonus Tip: Exclusively for your launch team (to save them that dollar!), you can choose to run a promotion a couple of days before launch with the book listed as free

for them to download, and then run a second promotion at 99¢ for the launch. However, you'll have to be careful so that you can still set up the 99¢ period the day before launch day so that there's plenty of time for everything to go off smoothly.

Alternately, you could do this the same way as the free strategy with the free days being private, but if so Amazon will not display the price as a promotional discount. It will simply be displayed as the buy price.

Once launch day arrives, share, share, share! Let everyone know the book is 99¢ and emphasize it's for a limited time.

Here, you can also share milestones and watch out for that shiny orange 'Best Seller' banner on your book page. That's something you can use for life! Plus, it'll feel amazing to say, "I'm an Amazon best-selling author."

This strategy is also a great strategy if you already have an audience but want to do something special just for your readers.

I mentioned that for the free strategy also, and you can do either, but if you have an email list of your readers, you can reach out to them on launch day letting them know your new book is out and it's on a special 99¢ discount for your readers.

Invite them to grab the book while it's at the special price, and make sure to let them know it'll only be available for a limited time. I recommend choosing one to three days for the promotion.

Bonus Tip: When emailing your list, if you set up the link to the book as a trigger link in your email provider, you can also set up an automated email sequence. That way you can reach out in a few weeks to anyone that clicked the link, ask them if they have had a chance to read the book, and invite them to share their feedback as an honest review.

You can even make the review page link in that email another trigger link, so that if anyone does not click the link, the sequence will reach out to them a couple more times to ask for their feedback. By doing so, you'll continue to get reviews for your book after the launch is over, which will further sustain momentum.

The Author Takeover Strategy

This strategy is a great one if you've got several established author friends or are part of a community, but don't have a large audience yet yourself.

The focus with this strategy is on partnership and the opportunity to help others while also getting in front of tons more people than you would just on your own.

This strategy can also be combined with the free or 99¢ strategy as it's a great opportunity to maximize your downloads and reach during your book launch creating some fantastic momentum.

If you just want to focus on the one strategy, I would still recommend pricing your book low for the release and then bumping it up to the regular price you'll have it once the launch period is over.

A quick note on this strategy is that it is one that does not require a launch team.

If you choose to do an Author Takeover, first reach out to your writing community and authors you know to ask them if they'd be willing to partake in your takeover event.

You can gather as many or as few as you like, though I would aim for at least five. The event can be a one-day event, the day of your launch, or if you have lots of interested authors, you can make it longer.

Each participating author should choose a time slot during the event that works for them, lasting about an hour, during which they can present themselves and their work via social media, typically with video.

You can also provide any authors that haven't done a takeover before with some suggestions such as doing a reading, maybe a video talking about who they are and what they love about writing, doing a giveaway of one of their books, or any ideas you might have of something interesting for readers.

Once you've gotten your participants, set up an event on Facebook. At the top, you can list your book and announce its release, as well as your participants in the description.

Afterward, share your event up until your launch day to get as much interest as you can. Invite your participants to share with their audiences as well!

On the day of the event, you can open the first hour announcing your book and welcoming everyone to the event. You don't have to take an hour, unless you want to, but afterward, you can post throughout the day announcing each author as they come on, as well as thanking the exiting author.

Not only is this a fun way to celebrate others and give their readers a chance to engage with and learn about them, but it helps you gain exposure and gain some readers that may not otherwise have known about you!

The Traditional Approach

Even if you're self-publishing, you might still want to take a traditional approach to your book launch if you've already made a name for yourself or have a large audience of potential readers.

The reason I mention this is that, while you might just want to go with a publishing house, the benefit to publishing yourself is the control and flexibility you'll have over both your book and your earnings.

After being both self and traditionally published, I do advocate for self–publishing, though there are benefits to working with a traditional publishing house.

One thing to note is that if your heart is set on traditional publishing, yet you want an edge when submitting queries, you can use self-publishing to build your audience which can be a boost for you. Letting your potential agent or publisher know you have an 'x' sized audience which will result in a certain amount of sales for the book can definitely position you well amidst all the letters in their inbox.

I'm not deep-diving in this book on traditional publishing itself, but let's look at this approach in particular for a self-publishing author.

As I mentioned, this strategy is best for those with an existing audience. With the traditional approach, the focus is on media and exposure rather than book downloads, though of course massive exposure will naturally lead to book sales.

With an existing audience, your first step once the book is published will be reaching out to them and sharing information about your book, as well as how it will benefit them as part of your community. This is especially true for business books or other non-fiction material.

Before the publication, it's critically important to begin scheduling media appearances, whether that be podcasts, radio, newspaper or magazine articles, or TV, as much in advance as possible. Ideally, you want to start reaching out anywhere from one to three months in advance to make sure everything is scheduled and ready to go.

When reaching out to media channels, having an established reputation does help immensely, as does having a news-worthy story you can tie into your book to make it an easier sell to media outlets.

If you already have connections with some media channels or have been featured before, you should feel confident reaching out. However, if PR is uncharted territory for you, you can definitely ask in your writing community for tips or advice or, you might consider hiring someone to help you with proposing and setting up these appearances.

For your already existing audience, you could consider doing a very brief promotional price, though as your focus will be on media and exposure, you'll be reaching a wide audience that will be buying your book because of all of the attention – and they want to be in the know – rather than because it's a bargain. So, feel free to price your book at its regular price point!

For this specific strategy, I am in no way guaranteeing you'll see massive downloads from doing all the media exposure. However, it is a great way to build your author name and audience, so it is a long-game type of approach.

Another important thing to consider is your budget if you're choosing this approach since you may have to travel and have other costs involved. So, you definitely want to plan well in advance. This strategy is meant to be very focused, scheduled, and intentional, so you'll want to take into consideration all aspects before diving in.

Ultimately, your strategy will depend on your end goals both for your book and yourself as an author. Regardless of which strategy you use, you should always view your book launch as an opportunity to connect with your audience and readers, as well as to continue to grow your community.

In doing so, you'll gain a larger and larger reach as an author, whether that be for a business or for your future books, which equates to more sales and of course more impact.

I am sincerely looking forward to your launch and your success, so I hope that you'll reach out to me and share all about it once you cross that line! (You can reach out to *katelyn@wewritebooks.com*.)

Key Takeaways from the Chapter:

- The primary book launch methods include:
    o The free strategy
    o The 99¢ strategy
    o The author takeover strategy

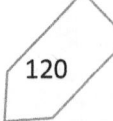

- The 'traditional' method
- The book funnel launch (see the Additional Resources page for more on this).

❋ Choose the strategy you feel you can most effectively implement and can commit to sticking through 100% till completion.

❋ Take it one step at a time, and continually celebrate every win!

Next Steps
(Beyond the Launch)

Once your book is live, it's not quite over yet. Of course, in pursuing a book launch that sets your book up for success, the goal is that the book remains somewhat self-sustaining, which allows you to devote your time to more writing (or your business, if that's your goal).

However, book marketing is a fantastic way to really give your book that extra boost of momentum during launch.

Before I dive into book marketing, I also want to encourage you to keep the conversation going around your book as your launch week progresses and even after it's over. It's important to continuously share updates and milestones around your book. For example, you can share screenshots of your book after your first fifty downloads or of your first review.

Doing this has multiple purposes. The truth is, we live in a busy world. Even people who genuinely want to support you and your book get busy, easily distracted, and frankly they forget. Posting regular updates, milestones, and mini-celebrations brings their attention back to the current event: your book launch. It reminds them to get involved, download, and leave a review.

It's also a great segway to privately following up with any of your support team members who haven't yet followed through on their commitment. Don't be afraid to ask more than once for the reviews! Make it as simple and straightforward as you can. Provide them with the direct link to the book page and encourage them to leave even just a couple of sentences. It makes a difference.

As you're celebrating, sharing about your book, and launching to the world, I definitely recommend utilizing book marketing in some capacity. This allows you to get in front of readers who might not otherwise ever see you or your book. Book marketing doesn't have to be time consuming or costly, unless you want it to be. There are tons of great book marketing resources to help share your book with that wider audience.

Below, I've provided a list of some of these resources ranging in price so you can find exactly what works best for you and your budget.

Some services require having a certain number of reviews on your book in order for them to run the promotion, which is where your launch team will come in. However, there are also some great promotion services which don't require any reviews. I recommend doing some promotion scheduled to occur on launch day to maximize the number of people seeing your book when it first goes live.

When you self-publish, you can keep an eye on how sustained your book sales are from the KDP dashboard. When you start to see a dip or loss of momentum, this might be a great time to invest in some book marketing to draw attention back to your book.

Book Promotion Resource List:

https://www.readersintheknow.com/list-of-book-promotion-sites

Promotional sites often require the book be priced at a discount, so I don't recommend running promotions all the time, but maybe once every six months or maybe even once a year during anniversaries of your book's release can be a great way to celebrate and keep momentum going.

Another great way to market your book is using ads, though I recommend doing small tests first to see what works and to learn how to draw your reader's attention before going big on advertisements.

Running an ad for your book can be very profitable if your book is for your business, or if the advertisement leads readers to the first book in a series, as once they become a fan, they'll want to read them all!

One amazing benefit of working with me and my team is that you are provided a book promotion package on your launch day, setup for you, so you can just focus on celebrating your book! This also includes a special book feature and optional author interview to my community.

Whether you choose to invest in book marketing, or simply rely on your book launch and then continue to write, always keep your end goal as an author in mind.

Once your book is published and the exciting time of its first release is over, don't let your own enthusiasm fade. Whether fiction or non-fiction, if your desire is to grow a career as an author, repeat the process! It definitely shouldn't stop with only one book. Start focusing on your next one – soon to come.

You can also continue sharing great content with your growing community, whether it be material relevant to your book's topic, short stories, or fun excerpts from upcoming novels. The possibilities are endless.

Here's to you and your success as an author!

Your Invitation

Phew! We've covered a lot. (By the way, if you feel like something important was missing or you didn't get the guidance you were looking for to finish and publish, send me an email and let me know so that future editions can be as helpful as possible:

katelyn@wewritebooks.com.)

Whether you're just starting out or you've published before and didn't achieve what you wanted, if you follow the process I've shared in this book, you will have your book in print on your shelf with a growing audience of readers to boot. That's my goal for you, and as you reach new accomplishments, I hope you share them with me as well!

As you go through the journey, know that you're not alone. Get involved in a writing community and get a buddy (if you've not got those already).

Despite all the information here, maybe you're still feeling overwhelmed by the process or struggling with pushing past some of the roots of writer's block.

Wherever you are in this process, I want to once more extend the invitation to book a complimentary chat with me about your journey, so that we can create your personal game plan and discuss making your dream of being a successful author a reality.

Just follow this link to book your chat:

wewritebooks.com/chat

Resources and Additional Materials

Just in case, I've listed all the resources named or listed throughout the book right here.

Idea to Print Bonus Package, which includes:

- How to Write and Publish a Bestselling Book, 4-Day Workshop
- Write Your Book in 90 Days (or Less) Complete Webinar Training
- Bestseller Blueprint Complete Webinar Training
- The *Become a Time Master* Complete System
  - *Become a Time Master* book
  - *Become a Time Master Action Guide*
  - *Become a Time Master Year Planner*
- The Ultimate Publication Checklist
- Additional resources and training

Get the Bonus Package: *wewritebooks.com/i2pbonus*

Alternately, you can get the *Become a Time Master* book straight to your eReading device from Amazon:

https://www.amazon.com/dp/B075FGPZST

You can view all of Katelyn's books, including those published under a pen name, at:

www.wewritebooks.com

Author-Business Tools Mentioned:

- MailChimp: *http://eepurl.com/hkf5Xj*

- Wix: *https://www.wix.com*

- KDP Rocket: *tools.wewritebooks.com/publisher-rocket*

Book Funnel Launch Method Training:

https://www.peacefulprofits.com/one-book-millions-method

Book Promotion Websites:

https://www.readersintheknow.com/list-of-book-promotion-sites

Learn more about Katelyn and We Write Books programs and materials for your support at:

www.wewritebooks.com

Thank You

Thank you so much for reading! I truly hope you've found this book insightful and helpful if you've been struggling to take that step forward to finish and publish your book. I can't wait to hear from you about your progress, journey, and book!

Would you take a brief moment to give your feedback, so I can make this book even better? I'd love your honest review, and it would be so helpful!

Go to this link and click 'write a customer review' at the bottom of the page to let me know your thoughts:

https://www.amazon.com/dp/B07RWRJ6NH

Thank you more times than I can put on this page!

Katelyn Silva